Sage Was The Perfect Shadow
A Survivor's Story

Mona Krueger

Blessings!
♥ *Mona*
Is 53

ISBN: 1-46639-361-0
ISBN-13: 978-1-46639-361-5

DEDICATION

to survivors
near and far
may you believe what your eyes cannot see
and find hope

CONTENTS

INTRODUCTION

Being an English teacher for second language learners, I confess to being obsessed with phrasal verbs, much to the groans of my students.

I love the fact that one little preposition can change the meaning of a phrase dramatically:

one small word describing *so much reality.*

Think of the difference between running *into* a fire and running *from* a fire.

Huge.

I wish I had had a choice. My fire, the one that consumed me, pretty much did what it wanted to, without any say from me. The following pages contain my story, framed in phrasal verbs…

to go through

1. go through (p.v.) When people experience something, they
   go through it.

Sage Was The Perfect Shadow

Masked

Masks are either funny or scary, depending on the context. Mine was scary. For most, wearing a mask is a choice. I *had* to wear one after the fire. It was a serviceable brown color that kept pressure on my new grafted face to cut down on scarring.

Emotional masks are more subtle, yet just as real. They can either protect or keep others at bay. Mine let me hide the pain.

A concept that is masked is either deceptive or simply mysterious, like the whys of tragedy.

My own masking can be canvassed with a little history. It was 1982 and at 18 years of age, I wanted a lot out of life. High school had been a great start. My list of achievements sounded good on paper: class president, captain of the basketball team, co-valedictorian, homecoming queen and voted most likely to succeed. It helped, however, that I studied at a very small school where being an overachiever was fairly easy. Nevertheless, I was excited about starting college, exploring careers and navigating the world.

I knew so little and craved so much, but my quest was cut short Thanksgiving Sunday of my first semester. A few moments on an icy bridge changed everything:

the skid,
the sliding,
the impact,
the gas pouring out on me.

It is easy to toss out words like *shattered* and *tragic*, tougher to take them in and swallow them.

Deep burns.

Surgeries can heal them but scars are life-long. My burns were deep, and covered a third of my body including my face and hands.

Face and hands.

The most obvious and un-hideable physical part of us. And I wasn't just left with a few scars. I lost everything:
eyelids, eyebrows, nose, lips, hair, an ear and all my lovely skin and definition of features.

The medical world attempted to replace all of it, requiring intricate and diabolically difficult `cutting and pasting' of my own donor skin. Magnificent work done by skilled hands accomplished a lot,

but I could never be the same.

It's tough to live without a nose.

It took about three years after the accident to have mine reconstructed, and the process dragged out following the initial surgery. You can't hide not having a nose. Makeup won't cover it, nor caps or long hair. All the usual tricks go out the window.

The vulnerability is excruciating.

Shame is a powerfully deep hole in our being. It's hard to breathe when I think of not having a nose again or losing my wig in public, which has happened in the past.

I've often wondered how cancer survivors think about themselves when they lose their hair. Do they feel any shame? Does the potential temporariness of it make it less so? I have come to the conclusion that there is something pure and simplistic about a cancer survivor without her hair. It has this way of bringing out the beauty of her facial features. One can see the vulnerability but in a heroic way.

Scars just don't allow for that. My head looks like someone took a knife to Bozo the clown. Exposing it to the world in combo with my facial scars is something I have nightmares about. Subconsciously, I fear that still, even after many years.

Hiding what I can seems a necessity.

My pride hates pity.
Maybe that is the bottom line.

After my accident, I was stuck in the brown mask for two years and was so determined to gain some of my life back that I gritted it out in public. No one could stop me from doing what I wanted to do.

And in some ways I could hide behind that brown thing, the scarred Mona not quite revealed yet. Masking the emotional pain was also easy at first. I was still in survival mode, exerting just enough energy to somehow get through the day, but the toll caught up with me.

Everyone hides something.
We work hard at keeping it hidden.
The unveiling is unthinkable.
Staying masked seems like life, but what kind of life?

Unthinkables

We all have a few of those dreadful, unthinkable thoughts:

losing a spouse or a child,
quadriplegia,
massive brain injury.

Being burned was an unthinkable for me growing up.

Back in high school, I saw an interview on TV of a lady who suffered facial burns and I had to turn the channel. I couldn't imagine her pain and didn't want to even go there in my mind. It was too horrifying to contemplate.

But when the unthinkable happens, one is forced to respond. Years after my initial stay in the hospital, I wrote a poem about my hands:

Marshmallows
It sounded like…
marshmallows — no resonance but the loud beating of my heart
two white balls of fluff resting on the table

attached to my wrists
they looked so bright and pristine

Doc slowly beginning to unwrap them
white gauze rolling off in waves
the silence became shrill in my mind
an inward scream at the unveiling

White turning to red – splotchy
such a gentle man given such a brutal task
the pain came then – sticky – pulling
ever so carefully revealing what I didn't know
what I had yet to see of my losses

I gasped as the last layer jerked free
what would be saved?
I could type 100 words a minute...
gone

The sound of shivering – shaking
nerves raw – tendons exposed – movement stifled
so many questions – unanswered

Cope – hold it in
think of white fluffy nothing
breathe
just keep breathing

Rewrap them
give me new gauze and shade the truth from me
later
perspective will come later

Peace – maybe some day
soothe it all by oblivion for now

Survive
just survive.

I tried to be brave and clung to a variety of clichés like `I am just lucky to be alive' and `I'm still me.' And part of it was true, so true. It was truly amazing that I survived that fire and I was thankful. But an unthinkable future still lay ahead of me.

As I got deeper into my recovery I realized that I couldn't change the channel. The first time in the hospital it hit me, I was up slowly traipsing the halls and came back into my room. Stopping at the sink, I saw the damage in the mirror. I had been there a couple of months and the image shouldn't have been a surprise, but it was my first non drug-induced moment of truly seeing.

I panicked. A silent scream tore through me, followed by a shrill, thin wail. My nurse at the time wasn't very helpful. He was appalled at my subsequent hysterics, but the devastation had hit me.

Mona was gone.
And someone horrifying had taken her place.
Dead would have been less painful.

Being burned is like waking up in the middle of a nightmare and realizing you are both the monster and the victim.

When you think of someone, that person's face is right there in your head, either smiling or smirking or somber, but that is what you conjure up.

Images.

My image was no longer recognizable and the loss felt like death. I had no great beauty before my accident, but I was me. I fit in and received a measure of positive attention. The loss was overwhelming, and not only for me. My family felt the devastation as well. My sister, Jane, wrote this poem:

Mona, I remember
> *the last time I saw your face,*
>> *as it was.*
> *Cheeks that were round and fair,*
>> *eyes so soft and green,*
>>> *sage was the perfect shadow.*

> *An unusual gift,*
>> *this moment,*
>>> *sealed in my memory,*
>>> *unaware that tragedy waited,*
>>>> *like a rapist in the darkest of nights.*

> *I remember*
>> *who you were*
>>> *before it happened:*
>> *full of life*
>>> *full of desire*
>>>> *full of dreams.*

We said goodbye.

The sleet didn't cause me to worry.
    Now I wish it had,
maybe I would have warned you,
    how could I know.

The bridge had frozen,
    like your life, in a moment's time,
    throwing the car into a tailspin,
        and you into the dismal arms of fate,
            where fire came from nowhere,
            seizing you and leaving you for dead.

The walls in the burn unit
    were bright green.
        You heard my voice
        and reached for me,
            confirming my horror,
            that it was really you.
    I silenced the hurricane inside of me
        I wonder if I ever left that room.

We watched your agony,
    helplessly,
        while the insufferable pain
        took residence.
            Your screams
                still echo
                    in my mind...

Mona, I remember
    His strength
        carried us through.

The reminder on the ceiling
His cross is over you.

Janie

I vaguely remember that first month in the hospital, though I was conscious and coherent even with heavy medication. Bizarre dreams plagued me while I slept. I would find myself in far away places, wounded and bleeding, unable to get back to the hospital where I could be safe.

Waking up in a fog, I would try and focus on something familiar. Although my eyelids were practically swollen shut, the one thing I could always identify was right above my head on the ceiling. The lines of the metal slats formed a perfect cross right over me.

It was my lifeline in that place, a reminder that God was with me, somehow holding me up.

My faith had a foundation. The small town I grew up in hosted three churches. The Catholics and the Methodists claimed the north side of town, while the Lutherans held the south. My mom and dad were Lutheran and our family was involved.

My accident tested all of our beliefs. I had been a dutiful daughter who took that same attitude to my relationship with God, but rebellion stewed at times and I struggled with questions and doubts. College had opened new avenues of thought and I was in the process of sorting out my faith when the accident slammed into my life.

It tipped the scales
in God's favor.

Perhaps it was desperation but my heart cried out for life to the One I knew deep down was Life. I didn't have all the answers, but I clung.

Every procedure in the burn center brought fear and pain. These were the days of tubbings, when debridement took place without anesthesia:

a tweezers and a sharp scissors,
torture by small instrument,
pulling and snipping.

Washing the burned areas felt like steel wool on raw flesh. Grafts only take when the deepest bed of tissue still intact is reached.

The impact of those frozen, excruciating moments stick. They take up residence in our psyche and some are beyond forgetting, becoming a part of who we are.

I was barely coping day by day. And that had to be enough.

Though I was clinging to God, too often white fluffy nothing was all I could handle.

Sage Was The Perfect Shadow

Fizzles

Anger.

It was so easy to be angry:
at my body,
my useless fingers,
at the gawkers who didn't even try to hide
their negative reactions to me,
at my entire life derailed.

I didn't know what to do with this level of anger; never learned how to express it in any healthy way growing up. Burying it felt like the only viable option, but at what cost?

In some ways it fueled my recovery. I wouldn't let the collective `they' get the better of me. I was going to make something of what was left of my life if it killed me.

A big question was whether the anger was a secondary or primary emotion. It didn't seem to matter, however, in the middle of a rage that made me want to scream. I coped by escape: watch a movie or read a book.

It was easier to escape to someone else's life that was maybe dramatic, but with much less pain than my own,

and with a better ending.

I could lose myself in the darkness of a movie theater and get rid of my life for an hour and a half. But the second those credits started to roll, the horror of my existence jolted me.

The fire,
the scars,
the pain,
the ramifications…

And then I had to get out of my seat and file out with a zillion other people and pretend that I was just like them living a normal life that I could go back to.

I hated those few seconds of burgeoning reality. It was facing all over again my nightmare with the realization that I had nowhere to hide.

Talk therapy probably would have been helpful at this time, and being someone with a plan to change majors from journalism to psychology, I should have had a clue about that. The sheer extremeness of my situation kept me isolated. I was convinced that no one could possibly understand my reality and rebelled at watching someone pay lip service to helping me.

I disdained the unscarred psychiatrist who thought they could make my life better.

My world growing up had been full of individuals who believed they had only themselves and God to pull them along in life. It was part of my German farm community culture with its emphasis on self-reliance.

I felt like I had to hold up the world, that *it* would be ok only if *I* were ok.

As time went on I sensed the rumblings of emotion bottled up and forced myself to reach out and get some help. One of those `disdained psychiatrists' had called me a walking emotional time bomb in the beginning, but a coming explosion didn't seem to fit my personality at all.

Fizzling created a better image for me.

A lot of my purging came through journaling,
one bubble of anger at a time exploding on the pages.

My hands had healed enough to type, but never again would I be fast at it. My mind could still fly over the keys but my fingers couldn't keep up. Even at half-speed, I could vent and disperse the anger with no one to stop me. I knew God was listening. I figured He knew it all already and was glad I was finally doing something about it.

Giving voice to emotions long held felt like self-pity and part of it was exactly that.

But it was honest.

And it let me see that not only could I *not* hold up the world, I didn't *have* to.

I could crash, have a bad day and even expect someone to be there for me. I took a step away from utter loneliness towards community. And on a good day, it helped. There were, however, too many bad days where nothing seemed to touch that feeling that no one could understand my pain.

Twisted

Grief was the fuel of my anger.

And like the new grafts that in their maturing pulled and twisted however they wished, my grief was layered and wily and had a mind of its own.

With a big burn, scar tissue does whatever it wills. There is no controlling it. Pressure garments help somewhat, but in the end the doctors have to let it do its damage and try to go in and repair it later.

I resented that.

The first year my stomach was getting so twisted from thick scar tissue that it hurt to stand up. It would take many long minutes of painful stretching for me to stand anywhere near straight. It was like wearing body armor you could never take off.

The armor was a part of me, built into my skin.
Trapped.

There was no escaping it.

I hadn't given up hope on improvements but life had become a waiting game and my recovery slowed to a crawl. I wondered if quadriplegics ever got used to not moving. It must feel quintessentially wrong at so many levels.

Something primitive in me hates restraints. I want to move freely, like those gymnasts who get to flaunt their incredible mobility. Reality was dictating a different course and the pain of it was dragging me down.

My life felt sabotaged.

And the why question loomed large in my grief.
Such a twisted plot my life had become.

An enemy had done this. I had no doubt. Pinning it on God never sat well with me from the very beginning. His character is good and burning His children incongruent with it. Some things in life just remain a mystery. I couldn't answer the why question but I trusted that God was on my side and would bring me through the wreckage.

As for the pain, I resolved to take it one day at a time. There is a quote from George MacDonald's book, *Phantastes*, that struck me the first time I read it:

"Afterwards, I learned that the best way to manage some kinds of painful thoughts, is to dare them to do their worst; to let them lie and gnaw at your heart until they are tired, and you find you still have a residue of life they cannot kill."

A residue of life had to be enough to go on, because no matter
the plot, it was still my life

and dear to me.

Sage Was The Perfect Shadow

Glimmers

Meeting Dave gave me some perspective.

It was about a year after my accident in the middle of the waiting game. I was waiting for my skin to heal and the grafts to be mature enough to handle more surgery. Each repair had to slowly build upon the former. It seemed slow and endless.

I felt stuck in my little hometown with all of my friends either going to school or getting on with their lives. It's tough to hang around someone whose life has gone wrong. What happened to the girl voted most likely to succeed?

Success for me these days consisted of going to the bathroom without my mom's help.

It was easier for people to pity me from afar than to be a part of my everyday existence. I didn't blame them. It made me thankful for my family, that I had a place to be and loved ones around me who would never abandon me. And for my own sanity, I had to believe there were friends to be made out there who could relate to me.

Dave was someone who knew all about getting on with life after a devastation. His misfortune was a phosphorus grenade blowing up six inches from his face in Vietnam, permanently disfiguring him. By the time I met him, he was years into his recovery, married with two kids and seemed to have found a way through it all, which seemed puzzling to me. Dave had a purpose about his life as an inspirational speaker, sharing his story with students, veterans and the general public.

What made him tick? He was definitely an enigma, and the first person I had ever met whose facial burns could rival my own. His initial hospital stay stretched out four times longer than mine, though part of that can be chalked up to the 60's and early burn care.

The further you go back in time, the scarier it gets. Doctors used the old wet/dry method to treat burns. They would roll the bandages on wet, let them dry and then literally rip them off, allowing for dead tissue to be removed. It's a wonder anyone lived through the torture.

Part of Dave's talk revealed facets of his story that made me wonder how he could ever have chosen public speaking as a career. But here he was with this crazy job of meeting up with hundreds of new people every day. To my way of thinking, it would have been so much easier to hide somewhere, work a desk job, write books, anything other than facing the public and their reactions, exposing his pain to the world.

As I gained more insight, though, I realized he had chosen to follow a career path that had started before Vietnam, as a pastor. Pursuing his calling kept him going. It made me think of my own dream of being a foreign correspondent, and with it the realization that a remnant of this desire lingered somewhere in the back of my existence.

I still yearned to see the world, write commentary on it and somehow impact it.

Dave's impact was in his message of forgiveness, that a great love could cover

mistakes,
apathy,
anger,
tragedy,
the puzzles of life.

His wounds had become scars, badges of honor for a soldier sacrificing for his country. I gleaned a measure of perspective that fire can do its worst, but life out of the ashes can still have meaning.

The compassion in Dave's eyes, the knowing, spoke into my unplanned journey.

He made the waiting game seem a little more bearable. He was the best example God could have put in my path at that time.

Maybe I could still succeed at something.
A glimmer of hope filtered through my dark thoughts.

Sage Was The Perfect Shadow

Desperation

A desire to return to college consumed me. I lived for the day I could start my life again on my own. Two years after my accident, I chose a state university with thousands of students, hoping to get lost in the crowd.

Wearing the mask put a damper on that. While it allowed me to hide the new grafts that were still a work in progress, the shocked reactions I received from strangers were devastating. And I didn't know how to help them or myself.

One day in a fast food place near campus, wearing a pink fuzzy hat over my mask and sporting a huge purse, I ordered and paid for a sandwich. A wary clerk, who avoided looking me in the eye, handed over a dollar plus coins and exclaimed, "Here's your change, Sir."

Now this was the 80's. Men did not wear pink very often. Nor did they wear those European male clutch bags that pretty much from the beginning have had a zilch percent chance of catching on in the U.S.

I felt neutral, neither male nor female but some alien creature in between. Even age became an issue. People would take my scars for wrinkles and ask me about my grandchildren. I could be 20 or 80.

I preferred 20.

My identity streamed all over the place.

I knew much of the problem rested on my shoulders. How could I control anyone's reaction to how I looked? I had to become ok with the new me, and stop living in la-la land with an unrealistic belief that people could and should easily get past my scars and understand that it really didn't matter.

It did matter to them.

The physical wounds had healed, but my emotional pain was still raw and bleeding. I didn't know how to process it all, and felt like I just had to keep moving. Back on campus my major was psychology. My vacations were spent in the hospital for reconstructive surgeries. I wondered how long it would take for everyone at the university to see me, react and get over it. I had chosen the place for its liberal and crazy, 'open-minded' atmosphere, figuring I could somehow fit in. It was a nice thought,

but `open-minded' has its limits.

The mask, with my one remaining ear sticking out, made people uncomfortable.

I'll never forget the swearing day. I attempted to go to one of those festive football games in the big stadium with thousands of cheering fans and rowdy, often drunk coeds cutting loose.

Loosened tongues more aptly described it. Never had people been so forthright in their response to me. After a series of `oh gross' and other hurtful comments, I bailed; literally ran back to my dorm.

But only after I used some pretty bad language, rather loudly.

They weren't some of my finer moments.

Normally I'm not given to such swearing. My mother taught me that ladies exercise a little more decorum. But I was fighting for my very existence, lashing back in an attempt to extinguish the flaming arrows stabbing my heart.

Public encounters such as these started to wear me out and dorm life, with its lack of privacy, weighed on me as well. I received permission to live off campus with my sister. We found a run-of-the-mill place with annoying cockroaches, but life got easier there. I had a place to unwind and escape to when needed. The combination of a safe refuge and my sister's unconditional love saved my sanity that year.

I wish I could say it all got better, that I gave up the dream of wholeness, worked through all my issues and found myself anew.

I wish I could say the new Mona became a better version and I wouldn't even care to turn the clock back and have my face again. But I would be lying.

I wanted that with every fiber of my being.

Distance

Most people kept their distance from me.

I longed for friends and was surprised when anyone would make a tentative step toward me.

I knew why Dave and his story drew me, but why would someone take an interest in this strange creature wearing a mask...

Was it curiosity?
A savior complex?
Pity?
I came across as a nice person, but not that nice.

When I first met Nancy on campus, she seemed too cutesy and together to ever be someone I could relate to at any deep level. In my bitterness, I was pretty down on the beautiful people of the world whose lives seemed so easy, which was totally unfair but there you have it.

I, of all people, should have known better than to judge a book by its cover.

My first glimpse into the reality of Nancy's life came when I caught her eating burnt toast for breakfast. She had set the toaster out on the balcony of her apartment, cranked it on high and let the bread smoke until it reached charred perfection. She didn't even try to butter the thing, just started munching.

Her explanation for this unusual behavior tore the lid off some major issues in her life. Burnt toast was a natural alternative to the gobs of Pepto-bismal she took every day to soak up the acid in her stomach. The stomach ulcers resulted from the stress of her family life in the past and present.

All of her performance issues were coming to a head as a business major struggling with baggage and feeling alienated from the more carefree college students around her.

To my surprise, Nancy's family home turned out to be just a few blocks from the hospital where I spent most of my vacation time. It cheered me up to have someone visit me. We both struggled with ongoing issues, trying to hide our pain from the world. Her persona was as unreal as mine.

It is difficult to imagine how another person perceives us in life. I thought I was pretty open about my accident. But the force I used to come across normal and unaffected made a joke of my seeming openness. Reciting facts like it hardly affected me must have seemed strange for a gal wearing a mask. The absurdity was definitely lost on me at the time.

I had grieved too little for any real acceptance to show.

Nancy was pretty much in the same boat, hence the connection. We could hang out, share drivel and sense the camaraderie underneath it all. At some level we knew we both were hurting and wanted to make a difference in each other's lives.

The magnetic pull of woundedness gave us a measure of closeness, but any wound can build walls tough to breach and I certainly had my share.

One of my psychiatrists had written a book about long-term recovery for burn survivors. Did curiosity make me read it? It certainly wasn't very palatable at the time. He analyzed the coping mechanisms used by survivors who have been disfigured and theorized that shame kept them away from any kind of intimacy with others. Keeping people at arms' length was a protection against being rejected, but the alienation made the thirst for intimacy that much stronger.

Friends like Nancy, however, lessened the distance.

Linked

Needing an escape from seemingly endless procedures, I bailed on surgery one summer and went to Eastern Europe.

It was the summer of 1986, the first one after my nose surgery. I wondered if I could handle the travel but took the chance.

My sister, Jane, was dragging me on a pilgrimage, a continuation of the one she had begun three years prior. She had been on a tour of Germany following Martin Luther's historic path. The tour weaved through Dresden and ended up at a church dating back to the Middle Ages.

The structure of the church was black and gray on the outside, but beautiful once you got in the doors. The place made her think of me. After exploring for a while and then sitting down, she glanced up. An embedded cross ran the length of the ceiling, reminding her of the one in my hospital room, a goose bump link to me.

That is when she decided we had to visit the place together.

My first impression of the place was dark, a tall spindly configuration reaching high. It looked sad and desolate, situated along the bank of a river with blue sky behind its sooty spirals. The scaffolds caught my attention. The outside was being restored a section at a time. Like my own outer reconstruction, the process looked endless.

The inside, on the other hand, was inviting. I soaked in the warm atmosphere and wondered about the history of the place. A series of photographs along one wall caught my eye.

They captured my attention because of their content, each frame stark and vivid. This church had been burned, and not just once. I stared at them for a long time.

I felt those pictures:
the charred remains,
the smell,
the devastation,
the loss of something precious

and it happened so quickly

no time to react
so fast
everything gone.

Ashes.

All my hopes.
All my dreams.

Step by step the photographs revealed the reconstruction. It was a monumental task. The carpenters focused more on the inside than the outside, the black soot a testimony to that.

The whispers in my heart began. Beauty of soul or beauty of appearance? I couldn't have both but which one was more precious? I knew the answer.

I had to start living the answer.

Sage Was The Perfect Shadow

Cocooned

Collegiate life suited me.

My schedule allowed for breaks when I felt the need to retreat to my dorm room to hide and recoup my energy. Success became tied to my academic performance. Getting straight A's allowed me to regain a sense of accomplishment, the one thing that had always driven me. I had something to prove.

I may have looked damaged beyond repair, but I still had a brain.

I was moving on.

1988. Graduation. With honors.

Such a long awaited event, six years and 25 surgeries in the making.

My family and the precious new friends I had made on campus were in attendance. A small cheer went up when my name was called.

I wore my cap and gown proudly, a tiny figure in the huge stadium, a sparkle of tears in my eyes, lost to the view.

It was a happy day.

When I was still in the hospital, my dad promised me a diamond if I ever finished college, a pretty unlikely reality at the time. I held him to it. A quarter carat set in gold, suspended on a medium-length chain.

I wore it humbly.

It takes a thousand years of granite pressure to make a diamond. Beauty forged by a heavy weight. It was a symbol and a promise. I was putting another facet of my recovery behind me, wanting to banish the lost years.

I considered college a safe place and for my next endeavor, I chose a small Bible College on the West Coast for graduate studies. I was a name rather than a number. Fellow classmates could actually see me once, react and get over it.

For the first time since my accident, I was in a supportive environment where it didn't feel like me against the world. I had planned to be there one year but I turned a certificate into a Masters in Pastoral Studies and stayed two.

Our spiritual life class was taught by the founder of the school, a man in his 90's. One day he was lecturing on how God will never give us more than we can handle. A burst of sarcastic anger rose up in me. It turned out to be one of those aha moments I will never forget, exposing buried rage. It was the impetus I needed to start seeing a counselor, to deal with more of my grief.

And it gave me a chance to wrestle with the whys as well. I gained the perspective that in the battle for good or evil, sometimes evil wins and God is left picking up the pieces, but with power and a promise, to bring something worthwhile out of it.

Beauty for ashes.
Strength for despair.

Would I trust Him for this?

These were the thoughts that stayed with me and went deep into my psyche. It was a big step to fully trust God for the new reality I was living.

Paradoxically, faith is something intangible, and yet solid, nebulous but a foundation that anchored me to Him.

Another graduation. Another accomplishment.

I felt stronger, both emotionally and spiritually, when the program ended, built up by caring people who saw potential in me. The world beckoned, coaxing me out of my college cocoon.

And I was scared.

to go around

1. go around (p.v.) When people or things follow an indirect or curved path in order to avoid an obstacle or to change direction, they **go around** or **go around** the obstacle.

2. go around (p.v.) When you **go around** in a certain condition or **go around** doing something, you go to various places and allow other people to see you.

Grit

I blame my sister for my years overseas. That trip to Dresden had opened my eyes to a larger world and within three years after graduation, in 1993, I was on a plane to Russia.

But my time there probably had more to do with the continuous gnawing need to make some sense out of my life.

Maybe I thought to escape the obstacle of my own culture and its worship of beauty.

Or maybe what spurred me on was the drive to see more of the world like I would have done as a journalist.

Whatever the subconscious reasons, I had this feeling that God wanted me to be there for a while and so the adventure began.

'The adventure' became the code phrase that wrapped all the good and bad parts into it, and my analysis of the place began the day I arrived and continued for 12 years. My pondering led me to the conclusion that Russia is one huge story of survival.

As I studied the history, culture and language, I caught on to
their grit,
camaraderie,
loyalty,
toughness,
appreciation for the little things and
a drive to make do.

These general characteristics reminded me of my friends from
the burn center. It makes sense when you think of all that Russia
has been through, a thousand-plus-year history of being
conquered, murdered and often abused. Suffering is in their
psyche and loyalty to the Motherland forged because of it.

The country has a lot to grieve.

In World War II alone they lost more than 20 million souls, a
truly incomprehensible number. After 9/11, I remember
thinking how agonizingly long it took to read the almost three
thousand names of those who had died at the first anniversary
memorial. Millions does not even compute. But I knew that if I
was going to understand even a glimmer of the culture, I had to
get my mind around the basics of their history.

My first city, Volgograd (the former Stalingrad), is famous as the
setting for one of the definitive battles of World War II. The
Russians stopped the Germans at the Volga River by sheer
courage and the sacrifice of blood shed. The city remembers its
fallen and commemorates them with memorials and designated
holidays. One of the traditions for any wedding day is to lay
flowers at the eternal flame in honor of the heroes.

I arrived in Volgograd with a group of Americans as a ι
After *perestroika*, the time of rebuilding following the falι
communism, we were invited by the ministry of educatio
some consulting work in the schools. Fortunately, we work ͜u
with interpreters because my initial language skills were nil. I
asked one of them to find out if a burn center existed in the city.

My first impression of a Russian hospital was not encouraging.
The burn center was overcrowded, dingy, antiquated. A foul
smell hit you in waves as you entered.

The doctors had skill but limited resources, which meant a
person's chances of surviving extensive burns were slim. I
received permission to visit patients but found out it was an
unusual request. Family and close friends were allowed, but not
strangers.

Thus began my knocking on doors, and the reception I received
varied. Mistrust was the most common reaction, but if I could
prove quickly that I wasn't peddling some cult or pushing a
wonder cure, the doors opened.

Being naturally shy, I had to force myself to go every week and
risk the potential rejection. I went because I knew the power of
camaraderie among burn survivors.

Sonia was a ten-year-old girl brought in from a village clinic.
She and her friend, Lena, had thrown a match into an old tank
on the orphanage grounds where they lived. It exploded,
catching them both on fire.

They didn't even attempt to save Lena, but they took a chance on Sonia. Maybe it was the life in her eyes or the spunky smile she managed, even with burns over 50 percent of her body.

That smile could con a hardened criminal.

And grit was her middle name.

The initial surgeries did not go well, which eventually sealed her fate. Extraordinary measures were not available for a poor orphaned girl. She had no bribes to give for the specialty bed or the expensive antibiotics.

I watched her deteriorate and tried to be an advocate, helper, big sister. But I didn't understand all that took place behind the scenes. The ward had one Clinitron in a private room, a sand bed that distributed pressure more evenly for wounded skin. Three months into her hospital stay, a new doctor took over and fought to get the bed for her as a last chance effort.

Renewed hope made her fight even harder to live. For whatever reasons, her stint on the bed did not last long. After her next surgery, she woke up in a room with five other patients all crowded together and knew that they were giving up on her. A poem I wrote describes some of the trauma:

The Common Room

I remember the way betrayal flashed
out of your deep sad eyes
to wake up in a common room
with all hope gone
people chattering around you

in that narrow space
dull lifeless droning ringing in your ears
chanting a death knell

You didn't shed a tear —
but the way you looked at me
those dark pools haunt me still
what could I have done to give you life
incompetent, neglectful, absurd
words that describe your caretakers
those who were supposed to be your advocates
useless all

I was no better
who watches out for such as these
lost children with suffering eyes
the orphans of the world

The bonds of sisterhood
should have been less naïve
where was wisdom in that crowded room
you knew they had given up
too many mistakes had been made
failure

How can I tell you my sorrow
the part I played was of one so floundering
I didn't understand the systems in place
I let you down just as they

Too late — much too late
I wish the clock were turned back and
I could have stopped you in that yard

with your friend
lighting that match…

You would be a woman now
embracing life instead of death

Sonia lived a grueling seven months. I have never seen anyone suffer like she did. Much of the donor skin sites they had used during the course of her stay never healed and these areas became worse than the original burns.

Her body was half decayed when she died.

Maybe her death would have been quicker and less painful if my presence there hadn't spurred the doctors to try harder. In my attempts to support her, had I only prolonged her suffering? It was a terrible question that haunted me; the naïve, do-gooder American trying to grasp and influence a corrupt, flailing medical system.

Sonia had wanted to live so desperately, even on the day they threatened to cut off her legs.

Her favorite story was of Daniel from the Old Testament. Daniel had been betrayed and thrown into a pit of lions to be ravaged for his punishment. God kept him safe through a very long night. Sonia had been waiting for God's deliverance, too. It didn't come the way she had hoped, but it came. I pictured her in a better place,

pain-free,
whole,
laughing,

walking with God.

And I had hope that I would see my precious friend again some day.

Merrymakers

After Sonia's death, a sense of futility hovered. I was being
bombarded with suffering at a scale I had never seen before.
Each of the patients I met at the burn center had their own story,
the commonality being wounds and those unanswered,
haunting questions of why.

There was the gal
who lost her hands in a steam machine;
the beauty queen
whose rejected suitor paid a mafia thug to douse her face with
acid, blinding her for life;
the grandmother
who was tortured with a hot iron to give up the money
supposedly hidden in her home.

I encountered a seemingly endless litany of tragedy and cruelty.

The power of camaraderie seemed insignificant too often, yet I
had to believe a listening ear offered something.

Outside of the hospital, I was treated like a guest, a foreigner, a curiosity. To a lot of Russians, Americans are perceived as shallow with our fake smiles and easy successes. We haven't been around the block long enough to have earned a true place in the world and so we are not taken very seriously. Basically, we have no depth in their eyes.

But those barriers seemed to fade when I walked into the hospital. One look and they knew I had insight that extended far beyond culture and citizenship.

In 1996 I moved to Krasnodar, a city southwest of Volgograd. The burn center in this city was far better equipped than the one in which Sonia died. The director gave me permission to visit patients for psychological care.

During Christmas break, 1998, my interpreter, Anya and I headed there to spread a little holiday cheer. We brought a guy with a guitar to sing a few carols. The plan was to go from room to room, but we arrived to find all of the beds pulled out into the hallways. The maintenance men were spraying to kill the cockroaches, so we had a big captive audience who welcomed us.

It was a sweet time and we sang to smiling faces and clapping. We left feeling good, only to be stopped by the director on our way out of the ward. He had gotten complaints from the staff and scolded us for `merrymaking in a serious place.'

I was stunned that professionals would have so little understanding of the psychological aspects of recovery. Did they not realize how much internal motivation it took to live through burns? To lighten the burden and focus on something cheerful for 20 minutes was doing harm? I didn't know how to react. We mumbled some apology and left feeling weighed down.

I pondered the experience and tried to analyze the director's reaction. Russians love holidays. They create feasts, make their own flavored vodkas and talk and sing long into the night. I theorized there was some rigid line between work and home that couldn't be crossed. Maybe the stress of their jobs was so high that it was impossible to think beyond it. If I could relate 100 sad stories of people I had met, some who lived and some who died, their repertoire was far greater.

I couldn't change their attitude, but I vowed to never get so hardened by futility that there was no place for joy.

Maneuvers

Needing to go deeper into this new environment, I signed up for Russian lessons at the state university in Krasnodar and ended up teaching English in a unique American studies department.

Being a poor negotiator with limited language skills, I found myself paying a lot more to study than I was receiving as a teacher, but that was in large part due to the International Dean of Students. A former KGB agent, he was crafty and ruthless enough to take advantage of a little American lamb like me. I managed a few concessions as the years went on, but knew I was badly outmaneuvered time and time again.

Control was an issue I often bumped up against.

One sign of it was the disconcerting lack of viable exits at the university that made panic rise up in me. The front façade consisted of a row of glass doors, all padlocked from the inside save one. I counted three or four doors off of the stairwells in the various wings and breathed a sigh of relief to see some emergency exits, until I noted the padlocks on them as well.

With the ground floor windows covered in bars, I shuddered to think of some maintenance man shuffling through a huge ring of keys in a dark entryway with fire and smoke filling the place, thousands of students behind him screaming and pushing to get out.

The thought kept me up at night.

I worked on the fourth floor, three doors down from a chemistry lab, without a fire escape in sight. With my own control issues creeping in, I bought a long rope and tied knots in it for my classroom. The plan was to tie the rope to a bar near the window and let each student climb down. It could work if we had time and no one panicked.

The last place I wanted any of us to end up was at a Russian burn center with the old wet/dry method of burn care still in place.

My students had never encountered someone like me before. I could see the puzzlement, shades of pity and skepticism in their eyes the first class. The fact that I was a native English speaker and the token American in the building, helped redeem me in their eyes.

The desire to learn English superceded their discomfort. But I had to remember that people burned as badly as me are a rarity in most places in the world and sitting in my classroom was an educational experience for them in more ways than one. Most handicapped people were hidden away by their families or stuck in institutions. The communist system thought them shameful, and even with a new era beginning after the fall, the old trends and prejudices would take time to change.

And that became one of my goals, to pave the way for the next handicapped person to come along.

I was paving the way every day,
on the streets,
in the trams,
wherever I went the stares followed me.

Some days I longed for some protection. My friends were mostly too short to be of any service, but on the trams I could throw up an arm and grab the overhead bar, maneuvering my body to block the gawks. On good days, I deemed it a game, but on bad days, a burden. I had no control over people's reactions to me. As always, the only thing I could control was my own response.

Camaraderie

The clash of cultures was never more evident than in my classroom.

I grew up in a culture that favors individualism, thinking for oneself and following the rules. In Russia, I worked in a culture that favors the collective, thinking together and bending/ breaking the rules.

So much was different in their educational system: curriculum, choices, grading. Once a student is accepted in a department as a freshman, his or her curriculum is laid out. There are no electives, no offering of a class twice if one fails, no transfers to replace students who leave.

And because the university bases teachers' salaries on keeping as many students as possible in the program until they graduate, a shift of power naturally occurs. I could not flunk a student and giving anyone a bad grade was frowned upon.

We needed to keep them happy.

Professionalism to me meant not losing my temper in class or blatantly shaming students. I believed in letting them make their own choices and suffering the consequences for their failures. But this system did not lend itself to that end. Russian teachers yelled, cajoled and shamed kids to toe the line. It was the only way to keep the power balance in their favor. For the students wanting A's, I retained some classroom power, but for the ones who were content with just getting by, I had zilch.

Our department was controversial because of its monetary value to the university. We attracted American students and their dollars through a semester abroad exchange program. It was a natural fit where the Russian and American students could mix and learn from each other. A constant battle raged, however, between the director of the department, a tiny but feisty woman in her early 60's, and the upper echelon.

They could give us new students every year or withhold them. Shutting us down and giving our foreign students to a more malleable department was often threatened, but the director held all of the key stateside relationships to make the program happen. Without her, all those lovely dollars could disappear. Because of this, the pressure for our Russian students to do well was considerable.

We had to look good and if that meant allowing some cheating here and there, so be it. The collective culture barely frowned upon it, while I was having a conniption. I felt like I had compromised left and right to fit into their educational system, but turning a blind eye to plagiarism and copying was beyond me.

During a major exam, it was my will pitted against my students' mischievous little souls.

In America, I could have read a book, looking up once in a while to make sure no one had any questions.

In Russia, I was like a wolf watching for predators.

I needed two sets of eyes to vigilantly and constantly sweep the room. If a student asked a question, I couldn't look at them directly because it was the perfect opportunity for others to sneak answers back and forth. It would have been comical if it hadn't been so exhausting.

As in the hospitals, universities had a bribe system that was never openly discussed but existed nonetheless. In some departments students could pay for their exam grades. The staff gave a set price for an A or a B. It began to dawn on me that corruption was everywhere and it fostered an extreme distrust in official leaders. My students were not politically active because they saw no point in it. Conspiracy theories abounded because no one believed anyone in authority, especially news coming out of Moscow.

It carried over to their understanding of the U.S. as well. Everything we did became suspect.

Bombing Yugoslavia couldn't possibly have been about atrocities in Kosovo.
Fighting in Afghanistan had nothing to do with terrorism.
And on and on it went.

One of the main theories centered around land grab. The U.S. planned to annex these countries and Russia, in their weakened state, was next. I was dumbfounded when a colleague revealed this pervasive belief. She was stone cold serious and I felt like I had to let her down gently and not insult her when I tried to convince her that we really did not want her country.

As I began reading more Russian newspapers and listening to other media forms, I saw bits and pieces of this theory sprinkled in and it staggered me a bit that people believed it. It put a new light on their reactions to world events and our part in them.

Trying to grasp all of these cultural nuances was like waking up in Oz every morning with a headache. My brain was being forced to develop new neural pathways to grasp the intricacies, a fascinating yet grueling task. Being forced to think outside of the box had a payoff, but far too often no one gave me all of the pieces of the puzzle. As an outsider, I could be a friend but never a true comrade.

Rodina

Russians have a saying, *rodina yest rodina*. It can be translated several ways:

Where you are born is where you are born.
Your homeland is your homeland.
Your roots are your roots.
Your people are your people.

I can't choose one translation definitively because all of them are needed to fully grasp the concept. In 1999 a series of apartment bombings occurred in several cities south of Moscow. They would take place before sunrise while most people slept. Because of the construction, multi-storied buildings would pancake, floor upon floor crushing everything and everyone.

I remember vividly waking up every morning during that time, relieved if it was already light out and my apartment deemed safe for another day. Living on the first floor of a 15-story building had its good side and bad. I figured death would be quick but if not, the tall pile of rubble would work against a rescue attempt if the pancaking trapped me.

President Putin tried to keep a lid on the panic and vowed that these crimes would be punished. He said they weren't crimes perpetrated against the government but crimes against the *rodina*. His clever use of the word rallied support and gave comfort at the same time, fostering a sense of we-are-in-this-together. He was tapping into a thousand-year-plus history of collective survival.

Russians often asked me how I felt about living in their country, curious why someone would leave the U.S. when so many try to do just the opposite. It was a complex question but all I had to say was, *rodina yest rodina*, and they would be satisfied.

It conveyed that there was something missing, that my time in Russia was temporary no matter how many years I lived there, that my roots were elsewhere and therefore, my inner world a little out of place.

This wasn't the first time I had experienced the shifting of my inner world. Losing my identity was similar. I had grown up in a body that felt like my own where the world responded to me and I to it in a certain way. It was comfortable, familiar and rooted deep.

And then one day I woke up in a different body.
These are not my hands.
This is not my face.

My world tilted. My self-perception had to rethink itself.

Mona Krueger

I've adjusted
but I'm not home.

Sobering

Drunk men loved me.

I was tall, blond and seemingly without scars in their stupor. I ran into them on planes, on trains, at the post office, even in the stairwell of my apartment building. For someone who has been shunned by sober men for most of her adult life, the drooling and pawing kind of attention was a slam.

One of my encounters occurred on an overnight train to Volgograd. Usually I got assigned to a car with grandmothers toting huge quantities of apples or career women looking forward to 22 hours of uninterrupted catch-up rest.

On this particular trip I found three soldiers occupying my car, one officer and two regulars. The minute the train left the station, the officer cracked open a bottle of vodka and started pouring shots, of course daring the foreigner to imbibe. Russian vodka rates up there with rat poison to my taste buds, so his mulish pushing was lost on me.

By evening the bottle was empty and the officer lurching his way over to my bunk, aiming for my lap. With a string of `nyets' and some pushing of my own, I got him back to his side. Seeing my unease, the regular soldiers assured me they would keep him in line.

A few hours later we pulled into my least favorite spot in all of Russia, the smoked fish market.

The officer was now snoring peacefully and I hoped the sudden stillness wouldn't wake him up. My protectors blew that thought to pieces. They woke the guy up and dragged him off the train, slipping back on with two new bottles of vodka and several of the odious smelling smoked fish wrapped up in newspapers.

It was party-time, Russian style. If ever there was a night I wished the blasted windows on trains could be opened, this was it. It was like trying to sleep with fish guts under your pillow and the foul smell perked up the cockroaches as well. And did the officer really need more booze to sleep through the night?

After these kinds of encounters, my desire for a husband was squelched. But the true reality was that deep inside I doubted anyone existed out there who could see beyond my scars.

I became half afraid, though, that I was giving off man-hater vibes, closed emotionally to any guy who tried to get close to me. Flirting was a humiliation-endeavor to my way of thinking, with too much shame to risk the blatant pity I might see in a man's eyes.

I resigned myself to being alone, though I knew my worth. My relationship with God established it. Being single has its advantages, or at least it does when I am in the mood to be positive about the whole issue. The other times, the loneliness cuts deep and the absence of a life partner is one more thing I grieve.

Perspective

I have an adopted Russian family.

We bonded over sad stories and gobs of Russian tea. They lost a daughter, Dina, at age 13 and a day-old son, Misha, due to a heart defect. Dina had suspiciously developed symptoms of cerebral palsy after a routine immunization while an infant. Many parents send their handicapped kids into institutions in Russia, giving up all rights to them and dooming them to minimal attention in dismal conditions.

But my friends, Volodia and Natasha, are in the minority. They chose to raise and love their daughter for as many years as they had the chance, even if it meant reduced income, 24/7 care, limited social support and living with the stigma.

Not only did they care for their own daughter, they also reached out to other families and offered support. Their grass roots efforts developed into a network of contacts and opportunities, at times seemingly endless. With huge hearts and limited funds, they still try and do what they can.

One of those opportunities led them to a place Natasha had always heard horror stories about, a closed-to-outsiders orphanage in a nearby village where Dina would have been sent. Once a child enters the gates, they never leave. The grounds even contain a cemetery for its residents. What goes on behind the walls, stays there.

With gifts for the staff and residents in hand, Natasha and friends visited. The group was given permission to come on a regular basis, as long as the supply of gifts kept coming, too. I had the opportunity to tag along on one of them.

I call it the saddest place on earth, only because I haven't experienced anywhere sadder, though I'm sure such a place exists.

About 130 residents live there, the majority of whom are completely bedridden. There are no TVs, no books, no toys, no classrooms, no therapy rooms, nothing but beds and floors. The staff come and go. Some care, others just do their job for a measly paycheck and wish they could be someplace else.

Vadim is one of the lucky residents who can walk and has a grasp of reality, though maybe oblivion would have been easier. He saw his misery.

One day while in his room late in the evening, he heard someone calling his name. Looking around, he saw no one awake so he went to the window to see if someone was speaking from the courtyard. It was empty.

He heard the voice calling again. And then the voice told him to request a Bible from the church group. In no way inclined to ignore this mysterious command, Vadim asked. The team was happy to oblige, but it seemed an odd request from someone who couldn't read. Vadim was familiar with a few letters but the pages of words made no sense to him. With nothing else to do, he just kept trying and trying

until one day he was reading.

The staff had thought him uneducable and his new skill shocked them. Vadim found peace in that book and shared it with his roommates. The words inside had a life and power to them. With some help, their room became filled with

music
and poems
and caring,
and a measure of life not known before.

A member of the group, Pasha, visited solo from time to time. One day he sprung a few of them from the complex, an unheard of and usually forbidden adventure for Vadim and his roommates.

They piled in Pasha's van and set off for a spot along a nearby river. Pasha pulled over, wondering at the silence in the vehicle. Normally the group was pretty rambunctious and an outing of this magnitude should have caused great excitement.

He opened the side door, expecting them to rush out in delight.

Instead, no one moved.

They sat,
transfixed,
eyes huge,
tears pooling
and then overflowing.

It was their first sight of a river and they were overwhelmed,
almost frightened, letting the view soak into their minds. The
shock of it lessened and wonder took its place. For a few
precious moments they were free, enjoying the peaceful beauty
of nature, a whole untapped world in their eyes.

They hated the thought of going back to the walls, but their
hearts were glad for the river. No one could ever take that
adventure away. They could live on it for weeks and hope for
another that may or may not ever come.

My own prison paled in comparison. I was living a life full of
adventure. It was far too easy to take that for granted. I needed
to be more like them, appreciating whatever came my way,
despite the denied dreams and unfulfilled wishes.

Ripping

My friend, Natalya, rips hair out of women for a living.

She cooks up this sugary paste-like concoction on the stove, lets it cool in plastic and takes it to work at her salon. Whatever area needs purging: legs, bikini lines, pits, mustaches, one can be assured that her magical sticky stuff will do the trick.

Of course, suffering is involved.

Natalya describes it as therapeutic massage because the ripping stimulates the hair follicles, leaving one's skin relaxed. I call it exhaustion from a pain-induced adrenaline rush.

Her sadistic job aside, Natalya epitomizes the strong Russian woman who has had her share of hardships: divorce, losses, dead-end jobs, limited income and health problems. Her only family is a mother with the beginnings of dementia setting in. Some months Natalya can barely pay for her apartment, but she finds a way to keep going.

We were roommates my last year in Russia, the hard year. I felt doors closing all around me and pondered returning to the U.S. My emotional support system had dwindled to where I felt like I had mostly drainers in my life and few replenishers. Though my sister's support from afar was always constant, the distance was taking its toll.

Natalya was the last of the replenishers. We had met at a church, two of the older single gals who didn't quite fit the young and eager crowd. Natalya is a truth teller, plain spoken and discerning.

It is said that `there is chaos in the Russian soul.' Because of it, the country is drawn to strong, sometimes despotic leaders. Only the strongman can give them hope to contain the chaos.

Suffice to say, a strong woman like Natalya who calls a spade a spade would not be a great candidate for a leadership position that would challenge the strongman. Her heart was in the right place, but not being a yes-person ostracized her at work and at church.

The rejection was painful and made her withdraw into herself.

My leaving was another blow. She considered me her only true friend in the city, maybe in the whole world, and now I was being ripped out of her life.

I thought of her as a lifer, one of those friends who I would always remain close to despite distance and time. But it wouldn't be the same.

I valued her friendship. She wasn't embarrassed to be seen with me around town and tried to protect me from the gawks when she could. Her personality didn't let me hide emotionally and she challenged me to speak my mind instead of playing the victim.

My heart was torn.

But the adventure had turned into something else. I was restless. Sonia's death had motivated me to stay and try to make a difference, but my puny efforts now seemed futile.

Everything in me longed to be somewhere else and I began plotting my escape from a country whose clutches had sunk into me.

I knew it was more about me than them. A piece of my heart belonged there and the place had shaped part of the new me. But approaching mid-life had me wrestling with my inner world once again

and I was lonely.

to go on

1. go on (p.v.) When something **goes on**, it happens.

2. go on (p.v.) When people **go on**, they continue doing something. Sometimes on is repeated for emphasis.

3. go on (p.v.) When you say '**go on**' to people, you are encouraging them to do something.

Assets

Mid-life crisis is taxing.

You accumulate this life with the good and the bad, and it keeps going and going until one day you step back and evaluate.

You wonder if you are living the life you should be or could be. I didn't regret a day I had spent overseas, but transitioning back had its challenges and I wanted easy for a while. I knew I didn't have to be on a treadmill of doing to be ok about myself, but I also didn't know what I was coming home to.

Grad school sounded appealing. I thought about working on a Masters degree in Education or Social Work. Needing to save up money for school, I went job hunting. With a limited stateside resume, it was disheartening. I had a few interviews but no job offers.

I began to question my assets.

I finally found something, a physical job helping seniors relocate. It wasn't a great fit. My hands bled with minimal provocation and the dust from preparing old homes for estate sales hurt my chronic dry eyes.

Thankfully, a part-time ESL job opened up, less physically demanding for me.

Emotionally, it was tougher.

My first student readily accepted me and I was relieved to be off to a good start. The second group, however, a young couple from a Western country, took one look at me and walked out, declaring that I made them nauseous.

This private company had chosen not to discriminate and took a risk in hiring me. I was thankful for that, but also resolved that if I couldn't be an asset to them, I would walk away.

After a long weekend of pondering, I decided to give it more time. I began to pray for God's favor for each new student and tried not to be anxious. The rallying began in my head: I have worth.

All I could do was be me.

Within six months, I received a reward for being the most complimented teacher at the company. What was behind that I didn't want to analyze too deeply. Did I have to work harder than a non-handicapped person to prove my worth? Probably. That is a reality for anyone on the non-dominant side of the matrix. But it made me doubt that the business world could provide a long-term niche.

I wondered if my scars could ever work for me, be an asset in some setting. It was a huge maybe, but social work seemed a possibility. Always feeling like I had to somehow pave the way claimed part of my past, but did it have to be my future?

Ramblings

Getting involved in the survivor community helped me find my bearings.

The burn center sponsored a writing group through a local organization that gave us a chance to interact at a deeper level. I felt a little sorry for the moderators walking into the group, frightened to see our messed up skin, lost limbs and cynical jokes.

We are kind of a quirky lot.

I wondered if they had to draw straws back at their office, to see who would get saddled with us. Normally, we were gracious but we also have an edge. Perhaps we sensed that we were being watched from a distance, an experiment. The organization tried hard not to foster this kind of vibe, but it crept in once in a while. Or maybe we just perceived it in a paranoid kind of way.

We are an exclusive club and not a popular one. We barely understand our own journeys, so for someone else to grasp our essence is asking a lot. Each of us writes in our own way for self-expression.

I'm not the only one trying to make sense out of my life.

In honest moments the struggles come out, but also the pride we take in our recovery. We appreciate every small battle won. Some days I crave to be around them, needing to sense the empathy of a shared reality.

Several of them are great fiction writers, the more outlandish the tale the better. I, on the other hand, am at a loss. One would think a fiction lover like myself could at least make an attempt at it, but reality is my bent and I crave the purge. Reading my stuff out loud would make the room take an emotional nosedive, but the caring kept them from shutting me down. We would joke that it was all fiction, while I rambled on from a black hole of grief.

One of the group, Lonna, hates clichés. To her they convey a simplicity that does not exist in this mixed up world, too lazy in their attempt to express anything vital.

She encourages my ramblings.

Her injury came from sleeping too close to a campfire out in a desert. The bag became engulfed and she destroyed her right arm trying to put out the flames on her legs. A stroke complicated her recovery. It occurred during one of her procedures in the hospital. The burns were fierce enough of a battle, and then to wake up in a fog with paralysis joined in:

ghastly.

Lonna has written a book with the subtitle: `Surviving Your Survival.' I laughed when I first read it, but in a cynical, knowing kind of a way. Recovery is complicated and long. The physical takes priority, then morphs into dealing with feelings and perceptions for a lifetime.

We are not who we were.

A chaplain friend recently asked me what it's like to be a burn survivor. I penned these words:

Under the Cloud

Being severely burned is a nightmare you never get to wake up from...
The realization that your life will never be the same
You will never be treated again as a whole person
Smiled at
Flirted with
Accepted as normal
And worthy of a positive response

Always encounters are colored by deformity
Scars that hide the beauty of old
Diminish the spark and candor of emotions expressed
Lost in contusion
Buried under ropy tissue
That pulls and twists wherever it wills

The battle to reconstruct is life-long
There are no breaks
There are no true get-aways
My scars always go with me

Visible - Encountered
Never hidden
Always responded to in some fashion

Out of my control
As much as I try to pave the way
I can never predict
Can never know
Only cope
Each new day
Each new person

A life lived under the cloud
The residual nightmare
That can't or won't let me go.

Each season of life brings new aspects to my recovery that I hadn't anticipated. For this decade it is my eyes. Because of the skin grafts on my face, my eyes don't quite close, leaving some areas of cornea exposed. My eye maintenance routine involves putting in natural tears, sometimes every half-hour and wearing salve in them at night.

Every day and every night.
Without fail.
Staving off eye ulcers is a constant battle, one I intend to keep winning.

I've always had this thought that time was on my side as someone living with scars. When other women would start to have wrinkles, it would even the score and I wouldn't stand out so much.

Naïve of me.
Natural aging and scars are two separate realities.

The real truth is that I've learned to not keep score. When I want to compare my life to someone else's, I stop myself. That is *their* story. I can only live my own.

The same encounters with people that twenty years ago would have upset me, I can smirk at today, or at least roll my eyes at and shrug off.

I am more comfortable with who I am, inside and out.
I can extend grace.
Quirky is ok.

Resiliency is the social work term,
but my writing buddies would call it
surviving my survival.

Recycling

Because I have an older sister, my clothes were rarely new growing up. My mom did some sewing and created matching outfits for us once in a while.

There were the leopard dresses and the vinyl vests in the 70's. Jane got the blue one and I sported the bright red. Usually, though, I wore the recycled stuff and understood that it came from a practical necessity.

I have always been a practical person. It is the German farmer in me. Even today I like the thought of things being used over and over, changed, revamped, not wasted.

Our experiences in life ought to be like that.

I have noticed over the years how anniversaries can be joyous or painful or bittersweet. My friend, Natasha, who lost two children, mourns the date of their births and the date of their deaths every year. The cycle just keeps going and weeks before each date, the awareness of it looms. The date of my accident is similar, Thanksgiving Sunday,

Black Sunday to me.

I feel it creeping up on me when the leaves begin to turn. A poem I wrote sets the tone:

Leaves

I love it when
the sun is bright on red-tipped maple trees in the fall
that smell is in the air
the one that reminds me of crunching Wisconsin leaves under my feet
and a football game waiting to be cheered.

Apple cider, hay rides in the fields
and pumpkins smashing
all memories of a lifetime ago
when I was me
it has been so long
I look back with such nostalgia
and can hardly imagine what my life
would have been like
without that Thanksgiving nightmare

Would the sun shine brighter?
would the reds be redder?
what would me – be?
the foreign reporter I dreamed of? a mom? a wife?

I always thought my life had no limits
until the scars put the brakes on my possibilities

reduced my life to those crunching leaves,
in pieces
dry
flittering away.

I heard a lecture once about the cyclical nature of things,
the ebb and flow,
blooming and withering.

Women know about cycles. They are just a part of our lives.
Black Sunday was a day I dreaded until I took control of it,
planned it into my recovery.

I made it a free day. Anything goes. I get to feel whatever I need
to. I can be mad, rage, cry, shake my fist at evil.

I let the grief cycle up in waves and crash over me again and
again, for as long as it takes. Some of its tenacious grip loosens. I
write a new `reasons to live' list, find that residue of life the pain
cannot kill and go on.

Recycled pain.

I don't want to waste it.
It has changed me.
It shakes me out of complacency, keeps me humble, reminds me
to focus on the good.

Pilebusting

I am the pilebuster in my family. Savoring a freshly organized area soothes me.

Why it makes me feel so good about my life is deeply seated. Control issues wind through the vein of that particular maze-like mine of my psyche.

Give me the worst mess, barring structural damage, and I am on a mission. The bigger the piles, the sweeter getting to the bottom of them will be. You can throw in dust, cat hair, the recycling and nothing will phase me; except for maybe small moving critters. They would deter me.

The pretty things you can buy these days to organize what comes out of the piles are a pleasure. Not that anyone gets to keep a lot in the end, however. Purging is the major goal of all pilebusting. But what is left is the treasures, or at least the useful, nicely packaged and added to one's décor.

I actually enjoy the process and not just the result. To some that makes me a bit of a freak, but to others a hero. A little organizational euphoria is empowering.

I helped another of my survivor friends, Katie, clean up her studio apartment. Her sisters have me on a pedestal now. They were ready to call in hazmat.

The place seemed a little overwhelming at first glance, but pilebusters see the future. We started in one corner and worked our way around the room. The trickiest part was not tripping on the yarn the cats had tangled through every pile and piece of furniture.

Once we could see the floor again, the decorating began. We transformed the room into cozy comfort with pretty red boxes, a little black pillow and a tall red lamp.

It became a haven for Katie, a place she can come home to and take a break from her own recovery, now that her landlord no longer has grounds to evict her.

Safety.

Katie is a people person, a sweet young gal with a bigger than life personality. She was burned a couple years back in an apartment fire. We visit patients at the burn center together every week, I as the old-timer and she as the newcomer. We make a good team.

There is something about taking the chaos and containing it, managing it, living with it.

It is what survivors do.

And then the maintenance begins. We know a lot about
maintenance: the meds, gels, creams and regimes of after care.
Staving off infections is a constant concern; and taking more
meds to manage the current meds. The maze gets a little crazy
but we ignore it at great cost.

The treasure at the bottom is one more day
and maybe the chance to empower a friend.

Heaping

Peter and I are buds. For a lot of reasons he didn't get much of his life back after his burn injury. The suicide rate among survivors is high, even years after the initial trauma.

Peter almost became one of those statistics.

Until the intervention, when a group of us rallied around him to offer some support and encouragement. My survivor friends and I talk about the difference between scars for men and women. Men can often get away with them being `intriguing' and `manly.' They still glean a level of acceptance and even attractiveness that is denied their female counterparts. If a guy loses a section of his hair, he can shave off the rest and throw on a baseball cap. No one barely blinks an eye. Acceptance gained.

Severe facial scarring is a little more complicated and tends to level the sexes. Peter lost his nose like I did, only he never got a new one. The surgery it would have taken required good health, pristine living conditions and concentrated after care. Smoking and drinking were taboo, habits long established for him and difficult to give up without help.

But the sad thing is that he doesn't remember ever being told a new nose was a possibility.

He became a man in his prime, living in a long-term care facility known for being the place that elderly alcoholics are sent to die.

He allowed himself to be medicated into apathy and rarely left his room. It was less painful than trying to get his life back with twisted fingers beyond use, compromised lungs which make more surgery dangerous and facial scars that makeup won't cover. The stroke he had in the hospital affected his language abilities as well. And the list goes on and on.

But someone has his back now. We are trying to keep him from slipping through the system this time, advocating for additional surgeries, better healthcare and regulation of his meds. And more importantly, we are helping him feel understood, cared for and worthy of love.

I went back to grad school for that Masters degree in Social Work. I dream of a job that will allow me to help others like Peter, who are taken care of in some ways, but not empowered to get their lives back.

It hit home to me again that touching another's journey is like heaping blessing on my own pain. And the Peters of the world aren't just around the globe, but around the corner as well.

Hunting

I come from a family of hunters, crazy men who get up at 4:00 a.m. and tromp out to the woods in the biting cold of late fall. When my brothers first learned to shoot, they would bring home squirrels and skin them in the basement. My mother tried to make them edible, but however she cooked them, fried, baked or boiled, that goal was blocked. The taste still lingers, and not in a good way.

My friend, Sue Ann, recently went hunting for a new used car. This is more my kind of hunting. She found a cute and snappy red one and because it needed christening with a road trip, we headed off for the Columbia River Gorge one day.

We hadn't been friends long. I met her at O'Hare Airport in Chicago. The flight we were supposed to be on had been cancelled and we were scrambling to get on the next one out. We struck up a short conversation in line and then I headed to the proper gate for a three-hour wait. The gate listed was packed with people so I chose one farther down the way with more seating.

Surprisingly, Sue Ann found me there a short while later, though she hadn't been hunting for me. The gate number had changed to the one I was sitting at. Nice coincidence, if you believe in coincidences. I figure some friendships are just meant to be.

Sue Ann has a Masters degree in Creative Writing, a nice friend to have when one is working on a book. She also lives with ongoing pain, though a different pain than mine. Her agony comes from trying to protect a loved one, a plan that backfired. Now she is cut off from her dearest ones, waiting and hoping that they come to their senses. Nothing about it is in her control, but it is hard to grieve a matter that could change in a heartbeat. Hope keeps her from accepting total loss. It is a roller coaster of uncertainty.

Some of her friends think she should have gotten over it by now. They are tired of her sadness, but the pain lingers. Walking with someone through long-term problems can be draining. The tendency is to sugarcoat the problem and subtly demand recovery.

Defriending is the next step. On Facebook you can do it with one click, but most people are more quiet about it. The relationship dies a slow, practically unseen death.

I want to be a better friend than that.

Mt. Hood was at its most pristine on our trip along the Gorge. When you live in a place with a lot of rain, the sun is a cause for celebration. When you can't have the big things in life you long for, the little has to go a long way.

We were on a hunt for joy:
a gorgeous view
a shared smile
an ice-cold passion tea lemonade.

Hunting for joy is kind of like writing a reasons-to-live list, but it is more active, a step beyond.

And to search for joy that lingers is the least crazy hunting ever.

Epilogue

There is a clock tower out the coffee shop window where I write,
reminding me of the passage of time.

The clock is ticking toward something,
the illusive what-ifs
lost in the relentless forward
grief still nipping at my heels.

I think about heaven sometimes
where the twisted plot of my life
will finally be unmasked,
where I will lose these scars.

But I come from a family with at least one centenarian
making that promised freedom seem very distant.

So I ponder my existence
and the whys of my life creep in.

I've come to the conclusion that
scars aren't some destiny or calling,

just a reality that must be lived.

If my scars have caused me to reach out to others
in ways I never could have, then in that I am blessed.

There are some worlds you can't penetrate unless you are *rodnoi*,
some places you aren't allowed unless you carry the same
badge, the same shame.

The knowing is sacred.

I am privileged to stand beside the beautiful souls
who have crossed my path.
I see their faces, past and present, as they drift through my
mind.

Who could forget Sonia's sweet smile
or the longing in Vadim's eyes?
Lonna, Katie, Peter and others,
my comrades on this journey.

Together we don't have to be so scared
or so lonely.

I can make some sense out of that.

Mona Krueger

ACKNOWLEDGEMENTS

to Mom and Dad
I couldn't have gotten through
the early years without you

to Bill, John and Joel
thanks for being my champions

to Sue Ann
grateful for the fine-tooth comb

to Diane, Jane, Rob and Colie
thank you for all the support
and the tears you tried to hide

to Kel and Nanno
your prayers
to the Restorer of broken lives
made the difference

ABOUT THE AUTHOR

With Master degrees in both
Pastoral Studies and Social Work,
Mona draws on the experience of her injuries
to reach out to trauma survivors.
After living and working in Southern Russia
as an ESL teacher and humanitarian aid advocate
for a chunk of her career,
she is now living stateside and recently
co-founded a non-profit in the Portland area
dedicated to empowering survivors.

For more of her writing,
go to monakrueger.com

Or drop her a note at
mona@monakrueger.com

10083996R0007

Made in the USA
Charleston, SC
05 November 2011